Animal Peculiarity part 2

By T.P Just

~~~

I0435994

Get All The Books In The Series:

Table of Contents

1 Prologue

THERE is perhaps nothing extraordinary in the fact that man is wise and just, takes great care to provide for his own children, -shows due consideration for his parents, seeks sustenance for himself, protects himself against plots, and possesses all the other gifts of nature which are his. For man has been endowed with speech, of all things the most precious, and has been granted reason, which is of the greatest help and use.

Moreover, he knows how to reverence and worship the gods. But that dumb animals should by nature possess some good quality and should have many of man's amazing excellences assigned to them along with man, is indeed a remarkable fact. And to know accurately the special characteristics of each, and how living creatures also have been a source of interest no less than man, demands a trained intelligence and much learning. Now I am well aware of the labour that others have expended on this subject, yet I have collected all the materials that I could; I have clothed them in untechnical language, and am persuaded that my achievement is a treasure far from negligible. So if anyone considers them profitable, let him make use of them; anyone who does not consider them so may give them to his father to keep and attend to.

For not all things give pleasure to all men, nor do all men consider all subjects worthy of study. Although I was born later than many accomplished writers of an earlier day, the accident of date ought not to mulct me of praise, if I too produce a learned work whose ampler research and whose choice of language make it deserving of serious attention.

2 The Birds of Diomede

There is a certain island called Diomedea, and it is the home of many Shearwaters. These, it is said, neither harm the barbarians nor go near them. If however a stranger from Greece puts in to port, the birds by some divine dispensation approach, extending their wings as though they were hands, to welcome and embrace the strangers.

And if the Greeks stroke them, they do not fly away, but stay still and allow themselves to be touched; and if the men sit down, the birds fly on to their lap as though they had been invited to a meal.

They are said to be the companions of Diomedes and to have taken part with him in the war against Ilium; though their original form was afterwards changed into that of birds, they nevertheless still preserve their Greek nature and their love of Greece.

3 The Parrot Wrasse

Parrot Wrasses too are doughty champions of their own kin. At any rate they rush forward and make haste to bite through the line in order to rescue the one that has been caught. And many a time have they cut the line and set him free, and they ask for no reward for life-saving.

Many a time however they have not contrived to do this, but have failed in spite of having done all they could with the utmost zeal .And it has even happened, they say, that, when a Parrot Wrasse has fallen into the weal and has left his tail-part projecting, the others that are swimming around uncaught have fixed, their teeth in him and have dragged their comrade out.

If however his head was projecting, one of those outside offered his tail, which the captive grasped and followed. This, my fellow-men, is what these creatures do: their love is not taught, it is inborn.

The 'Anthia's'

As loyal men and true fellow-soldiers come to one another's aid, so do the fish which men skilled in sea-fishing call Anthias; and their haunts are the seas. For instance, directly they are aware that a mate has been hooked, they swim up with all possible speed; then they set their back against him and by falling upon him and pushing with all their might try to stop him from being hauled in.

4 The Gnawer

Of the fish known as the 'Gnawer' its name and, what is more, its mouth declare its nature. Its teeth grow in an unbroken line and are numerous and so strong as to bite through anything that comes their way.

Therefore, when taken with a hook, it is the only fish that does not attempt to withdraw, but presses on in its eagerness to cut the line. Fishermen however counter this by a device: they have their hooks forged with a long shank.

But the Gnawer, being a powerful jumper in its way, often leaps above the shank, and cutting the hair—line that is drawing it, swims away again to the places where fish haunt.

And Dolphins

It also gathers round it a shoal of its fellows and with them also makes an attack upon the Dolphins. And if one chance to get separated from the rest, the Gnawers surround it and then set upon the creature furiously, knowing as they do that the Dolphin is by no means insensible to their bites.

For the Gnawers cling most tenaciously to it, while the Dolphin leaps upwards and plunges; and it shows it is being tormented by the pain, for the Gnawers that have fastened upon it are lifted out of the water with it as it leaps. And while the Dolphin struggles to shake them loose and beat them off, they never relax their hold, but would eat it alive.

Then however when each Gnawer has bitten away a piece, they go off with their mouthful, and the Dolphin is thankful to swim away after having fed its uninvited guests (if one may so call them) to its own pain.

5 The Jackal

Men say that the Jackal is most friendly disposed to man, and Whenever it happens to encounter a man, it gets out of his way as though from deference; but when it sees a man being injured by some other animal, it at once comes to his help.

Nicias and his hounds

One Nicias unwittingly outdistanced his fellow huntsmen and fell into a charcoal-burners furnace. But his hounds, which saw this happen, did not leave the spot, but at first remained Whining and baying about the furnace, until at length, by just daring to bite the clothes of passers-by gently and cautiously, they tried to draw them to the scene of the mishap, as though the hounds were imploring the men to come to their master's help.

One man at any rate seeing this, suspected what had occurred and followed. He found Nicias burned to death in the furnace, and from the remains he guessed the truth.

6 The Drone

The Drone, which is born among bees, hides itself among the combs during the day, but at night, when it observes that the bees are asleep; it invades their work and makes havoc in the hives.

When the bees realise this (most of them are asleep, being thoroughly tired, though a few are lying in Wait for the thief), directly they catch him they beat him, not violently, and thrust him out and cast him forth into exile.

Yet even so the Drone has not learnt his lesson, for he is naturally, slothful and greedy-two bad qualities! So he secretes himself outside the combs and later, when the bees fly forth to their feeding-grounds, pushes his way in and does what is natural to him, cramming himself and plundering the bees treasure of honey.

But they on returning from their pasturage, directly they encounter him, no longer beat him with moderation nor merely put him to flight, but fall upon him vigorously and make an end of the thief. The punishment which he suffers none can censure: he pays for his gluttony and voracity with his life. This is what bee-keepers say, and they convince me.

Bees and their ages

A man may tell the age of Bees in the following way. Those born in the current year are glistening and are the colour of olive oil; the older ones are rough to the eye and to the touch and appear wrinkled with age. They have however greater experience and skill, time having instructed them in the art of making honey.

As Weather Prophets

They have too the faculty of divination, so that they know in advance when rain, and frost are coming. And whenever they reckon that either or both are on their way, they do not extend their flight very far, but fly round about their hives as though they would be close to the door. It is from these signs that bee-keepers augur the approach of stormy weather and warn the farmers. And yet Bees are not so afraid of frost as they are of heavy rain and snow.

Often they fly against the wind, carrying between their feet a small pebble of such size as is easy to carry when on the wing. This is a device which they use to ballast themselves against a contrary wind, and particularly so that the breeze may not deflect them from their path.

7 The Mullet

Even among fishes there are many kinds which know how strong is love, for that god, powerful as he is, has not ignored and disdained even the creatures that dwell below in the depths of the ocean.

One at any rate that pays service to this god is the Mullet, but not every species, only that to which men who have observed the different species of fish have given a name derived from its sharp snout. These, I am told, are caught in great numbers round about the Gulf of Achaia, and there are various ways of catching them. But the following method of capture proves how madly amorous they are.

How caught

A fisherman catches a female Mullet and fastens it to a long rod or a cord (this too must be long); as he walks slowly along the sea-shore he draws the fish, swimming and gasping, after him. In his footsteps there follows one with a net, and this net-fisherman watches diligently to see what is going to happen and where.

So the female Mullet is towed along, and all the males that catch sight of her, like (one might say) licentious youths ogling a beautiful girl as she hurries by, come swimming up, mad with sexual desire.

Thereupon the man with the net casts it and frequently has good luck, thanks to the urgent lust of the fish that approach. It is essential for the first fisher1nan's purpose that the captured female should be at her prime and Well-fleshed, so that a greater number may be ardent after her and may take the bait which her enticing beauty offers.

But should she be lean, most of them will scorn her and go away. Still, if any one of them is madly in love, he will not leave her, because he has been enslaved not by her beauty (that I will swear) but by his desire for sexual intercourse.

8 The 'Etna-Fish'

It seems however that fish are also models of continence. At any rate when the 'Etna-fish' ,as it is called, pairs with its mate as with a wife and achieves the married state, it does not touch another female; it needs no covenants to maintain its fidelity, no dowry; it even stands in no fear of an action for ill-usage, nor is Solon to it a name of dread. What noble laws, how worthy of veneration!
And man, the libertine, feels no scruple at disobeying them.

9 The Wrasse

The Wrasse has its haunts and resorts among the rocks and near cavernous burrows. The males all have many Wives and resign the hollow places, as though they were women's chambers, to their brides. This refinement in their mating, and the propensity which they enjoy for, having many wives one might describe as characteristic of barbarians who luxuriate in the pleasures of the bed, and (if one may jest on serious subjects) as living like the Medes and Per-Asians.

It is of all fishes the most jealous at all times, but especially when its wives are producing their young. (If by excessive use of these expressions I make my discourse too wanton, the facts of nature permit me to do things of that sort.) So the females which are actually facing the strain of birth-pangs remain quiet in their homes, while the male, after the manner of a husband, stays about the entrance to prevent any mischief from outside, being anxious for his offspring.

For it seems that he loves even those that are yet unborn, and it is his fatherly concern that causes him these early fears; he even spends the whole day without touching food: his care sustains him. But as the afternoon grows late, he relinquishes his forced Watch and seeks for food, which he does not fail to find. But of course each of the females within, whether in the act of giving birth or after it, finds a quantity of seaweed in the hollow places and about the rocks, and this is their meal.

The Wrasse, how caught

A fisherman who is skilled in angling a Wrasse fastens a heavy piece of lead to his hook, wraps round it a large prawn, and drops the bait. And then he moves the line a little, rousing and egging on his prey to take the food, while the prawn by its movement conveys the impression that it intends to enter the Wrasse's den.

Now this the Wrasse greatly resents, and therefore, as soon as he observes it, he longs, such is his fury, to demolish the object of his abhorrence, for he is not thinking of his appetite at the moment; and when he has-crushed it, he moves of, considering it more honourable and more important that the watchman should not be caught napping than that he should be fed.

But when he intends to eat any other creature that comes his Way, he crushes it lightly and then lets it lie. As soon as he sees that it is dead, then at length he nibbles at it.

But the female Wrasses, so -long as they see the male acting as their shield, so to say, remain within and with the care of their household are occupied. If however the male disappears, they become distraught; their despondency leads them to venture forth, and then they are caught.

10 The Blue-grey fish

Among fishes the "Blue-grey' is a model father. He maintains a strenuous Watch over his mate's offspring, to ensure that they are not attacked or injured. And all the While that they are swimming the sea happily and without fear he never relaxes his vigilance, and sometimes brings up the rear and sometimes does not, but swims by them now on this side now on that.

And if any of his young is afraid, he opens his mouth and takes the baby in. Later, when its fear has passed, he disgorges the one that took refuge exactly as he received it, and it resumes its swimming.

The Dog-fish

Directly the Dog—fish has produced its young, it has them swimming by its side, and there is no delay. But if any one of them is afraid, it slips back into its mother's womb. Later, when its fear has passed, it emerges, as though it were being born again.

11 The Dolphin and its young

Men admire women for their devotion to their children, yet I observe that mothers whose sons or whose daughters have died continued to live and in time forgot their sufferings, their grief having abated. But the female Dolphin far surpasses all creatures in its devotion to its offspring. It produces two. And when a fisherman either wounds a young Dolphin with his harpoon or strikes it with his barb . . . The barb is pierced at the upper end, and a long line is fastened to it, while the barbs sink in and hold the fish. So long as the wounded Dolphin still has any strength, the fisher-man leaves the line slack, so that the fish may no break it by its violence, and so that he himself may not incur a double misfortune through the Dolphin escaping with the barb and himself is failing to catch anything.

As soon as he perceives that the fish is tiring and is somewhat weakened by the wound, he gently brings his boat near and lands his catch. But the mother Dolphin is not scared by what has occurred nor restrained by fear, but by a mysterious instinct follows in her yearning for her child.

And though one confront her with terrors never so great, she is still undismayed, and will not endure to desert her young one which has come to a bloody end; indeed, it is even possible to strike her with the hand, so close does she come to the hunters, as though she would beat them oil'. And so it comes about that she is caught along with her offspring, though she could save herself and escape.

But if both her off-spring are by her, and if she realises that one has been Wounded and is being hauled in, as I said above, she pursues the one that is unscathed and drives it away, lashing her tail and biting her little one with her mouth; and she makes a blowing sound as best she can, indistinct, but giving the signal to flee, which saves it. So the young Dolphin escapes, while the mother remains until she is caught and dies along with the captive.

12 The Horned Ray

The Horned Ray is born in the mud, and though at the time of birth it is very small, it grows from that size to be enormous. Its belly beneath is white; its back, its head, and its sides are a deep black; its mouth however is small, and its teeth-when it opens its mouth, you cannot see them. Further it is exceedingly long and flat.

While on the one hand it feeds upon a great number of fish, yet its chief delight is to eat the flesh of man. It is conscious of its very small strength: only its great size gives it courage. Hence when it sees a man swimming or diving to catch something in the water, it rises and arching its body attacks him, pressing upon him from above with all its weight; and while causing terror to fasten upon him, the Ray extends all its body over the wretched man like a roof and prevents him from reaching the surface and breathing.

When therefore his breathing is arrested, the man naturally dies, and the Ray falls upon him and in the feast which it most greedily desires reaps the reward of its persistence.

13 The Cicada

All other songsters sing sweetly and use their tongue to utter, as men do, but Cicadas produce their incessant chatter from their loins. They feed upon dew, and from dawn until about midday remain silent.

But when the sun enters upon his hottest period, they emit their characteristic clamour industrious members of a chorus, you might call them and from above the heads of shepherds and Wayfarers and reapers their song descends. This love of singing Nature has bestowed upon the males, whereas the female Cicada is mute and appears as silent as some shame fast maiden.

14 The Spider and its web

Men say that it was the goddess Ergane who invented
Weaving and spinning, but it was Nature that trained the
Spider to weave.

The practice of its craft is not due to any imitation, nor does it
and weaves. It is so extremely industrious that not even the
most dexterous women, skilled at elaborating wrought yarn,
can be compared to it: its web is thinner than hair.

The Ant

Historians praise the Babylonians and Chaldeans for their
knowledge of the heavenly bodies. But Ants, though they
neither look upwards to the sky nor are able to count the days
of the month on their fingers, nevertheless have been
endowed by Nature with an extraordinary gift.

Thus, on the first day of the month they stay at home indoors,
never quitting their nest but remaining quietly within.

15 The Sargue

The fish known as the Sargue has its home among rocks and hollows, which however have in them narrow clefts so that the rays of the sun can penetrate within and fill these fissures with light. For Sargues like all the light there is, but have an even greater craving for the sunbeams.

They live in great numbers in the same place, and their usual haunts are the shallows of the sea, and they particularly like to be near the land. For some reason they have a strong affection for goats. At any rate if the shadow of one or two goats feeding by the sea-shore falls upon the water, they swim in eagerly and spring up as though for joy, and in their desire to touch the goats they leap out of the Water, though, they are not in a general Way given to leaping.

And even when swimming below the Waves they are sensible of the goats smell, and for delight in it press in to be near them.

How Caught

Now since they are thus love-sick, the object of their love is the means of their capture. Thus, a fisherman wraps himself in a goatskin which has been flayed with the horns. Stalking his prey, the hunter gets the sun behind him and then sprinkles on the Water beneath which the aforesaid fish live, barley-groats soaked in broth of goat's flesh.

And the Sargues, attracted by the aforesaid smell as though by some charm, approach and eat the barley-groats and are fascinated by the goats flesh. And the man catches them in numbers with a stout hook and a line of white flax attached not to a reed but to a rod of cornel-wood.

For it is essential to haul in the fish that has taken the bait very quickly so as to avoid disturbing the others. They are even to be caught by hand, if by gently stroking the spines, which they raise in self — protection, from the head downwards one can lay them, or by pressure draw the fish out of the rocks into which they thrust themselves to avoid being seen

16 Vipers and their mating

The male Viper couples with the female by wrapping himself round her. And she allows her mate to do this without resenting it at all. When however they have finished their act of love, the bride in reward for his embraces repays her husband with a treacherous show of affection, for she fastens on his neck and bites it off, head and all.

So he dies, while she conceives and becomes pregnant. But she produces not eggs but live young ones, which immediately act in accordance with their nature at its worst. At any rate they gnaw through their mother's belly and forthwith emerge and avenge their father. What then, my dramatist friends, have your Oresteses and your Alcmaeons to say to this?

17 The Hyena

Should you this year set-eyes on a male Hyena, next year you will see the same creature as a female; conversely, if you see a female now, next time you will see a male.

They share the attributes of both sexes and are both husband and Wife, changing their sex year by year. So then it is not through extravagant tales but by actual facts that this animal has made Caeneus and Teiresias old-fashioned

18 The Black Sea-bream

As men fight for beautiful women, so do animal's fight for their females, goats with goats, bulls with bulls, and rams with their rivals in love for sheep. Even the Black Sea-bream wax wanton for their females.

They are born in what men call rough places, and are jealous, and one may see them fighting vigorously for their females. And they do not contend for several, in the Way that Sargues do, but each for its own mate, just as Menelaus fought for his wife with Paris.

19 The Octopus

The Octopus feeds first on one thing and then on another, for it is terribly greedy and for ever plotting some evil, the reason being that it is the most omnivorous of all sea-animals.
The proof of this is that, should it fail to catch anything, it eats its own tentacles, and by filling its stomach so, finds a remedy for the lack of prey. Later it renews its missing limb, Nature seeming to provide this as a ready meal in times of famine.

20 The Owl

The Owl is a wily creature and resembles a witch. And when captured, it begins by capturing its hunters. And so they carry it about like a pet or (I declare) like a charm on their shoulders. By night it keeps watch for them and with its call that sounds like some incantation it diffuses a subtle, soothing enchantment, thereby attracting birds to settle near it.
And even in the daytime it dangles before the birds another kind of lure to make fools of them, putting on a different expression at different times and all the birds are spellbound and remain stupefied and seized with terror, and a mighty terror too, at these transformations.

Get All The Books In The Series:

Animal Peculiarity: Part 1
Animal Peculiarity: Part 2
Animal Peculiarity: Part 3
Animal Peculiarity: Part 4
Animal Peculiarity: Part 5
Animal Peculiarity: Part 6
Animal Peculiarity: Part 7
Animal Peculiarity: Part 8

.